HELICOPTERS

MARK DARTFORD

Lerner Publications Company
Minneapolis

First American edition published by Lerner Publications Company.

Copyright © 2003 by The Brown Reference Group plc.

Lerner Publications Company.
A division of Lerner Publishing Group
241 First Avenue North
Minneapolis, MN 55401 U.S.A.

Website address: www.lernerbooks.com

Library of Congress Cataloging-in-Publication Data

Dartford, Mark.
 Helicopters / by Mark Dartford.
        p. cm.—(Military hardware in action)
Includes index.
Summary: Describes various models of helicopters used for military purposes, from the Sikorsky to the A160 Hummingbird.
  ISBN 0–8225–4707–4 (lib. bdg.)
 1. Military helicopters—Juvenile literature. [1. Military helicopters.
2. Helicopters.] I. Title. II Series.
  UG1230 .D37 2003
  623.7'43047—dc21   2002011855

Printed in China
Bound in the United States of America
1 2 3 4 5 6 – OS – 08 07 06 05 04 03

This book uses black and yellow chevrons as a decorative element on some headers. They do not point to other elements on the page.

Contents

Introduction

The oncoming sound of spinning rotor blades fills the evening air. Soon a dozen black dots, low on the skyline, grow bigger as the helicopters approach. Suddenly a stream of rockets and machine-gun fire streaks across the tops of the trees, causing panic and destruction below. The helicopter—slow and squat compared to fixed-wing strike airplanes—is still a powerful weapon.

INCOMING

Bell UH1 Hueys swoop down on a low-level mission in Vietnam during the 1960s.

Art, Science, and Aviation

The idea of using a rotating wing to lift a person-carrying capsule off the ground is not new. The Italian artist and inventor Leonardo da Vinci came up with a design in the 1490s. Many people believe that his designs for a flying machine were hundreds of years ahead of their time. In fact, it was not until the 1920s that a true rotorcraft successfully lifted off.

FIRST FLIGHTS

A Spaniard named Don Juan de la Cierva built and flew the first successful **autogiro** in the 1920s. It was a small aircraft that used a propeller-driven motor to provide forward speed. It also had a free-spinning rotor to give **lift**. A decade later, Germany's Fw61 appeared. It was the first pilot-controlled rotorcraft.

DA VINCI'S DESIGN

Da Vinci's plan used an upward-facing airscrew. His design was never built.

GERMAN SUCCESS

The Focke-Achgelis was a helicopter flown from the deck of a World War II (1939–1945) submarine.

Sikorsky

In the United States, Igor Sikorsky developed the first military helicopter that could be made in large numbers. It had a single main rotor and a small **anti-torque tail rotor**.

HOVERFLY

The Sikorsky R4 was the only mass-produced military helicopter of World War II.

Korea

The helicopter made its real combat start in Korea in the early 1950s. It mostly carried supplies and wounded personnel to and from the battle zones.

EXPLOSIVE LOAD

An HRS Sikorsky helicopter hovers as marines load weapons into its cargo net in Korea.

Late 1900s

Helicopter (chopper) warfare came into its own during the Vietnam War (roughly 1965–1975). Vietnam is a mountainous country, and much of it is covered in jungle. U.S. forces used helicopters for active combat missions and all kinds of transport and supply.

DO-ALL

A wounded soldier is carried from an Iroquois UH1 helicopter during the Vietnam War.

PEACEKEEPING

Helicopters played an increasingly important part in conflicts of the late 1900s. These included the war in Bosnia (1980s) and **Operation Desert Storm** (1991). Choppers were also part of operations against terrorists in Afghanistan in 2001 and 2002.

DESERT STORM

A U.S. Army MH53 Stallion stirs up the sand in Iraq during Operation Desert Storm.

>> **Operation Desert Storm** = a 1991 war against Iraq after it invaded Kuwait   7

The Rotorcraft Role

Modern helicopters come in all shapes and sizes. They perform many roles. Anti-armor helicopters work on the front line, taking out enemy tanks and guns. At sea, helicopters are used for information gathering, antisubmarine warfare, and air/sea rescues. Large helicopters transport troops, equipment, and supplies.

TANK BUSTER

The AH1 Cobra is a proven attack helicopter. It is equipped with tube-launched TOW missiles. It carries out short-range, low-level strikes against individual enemy targets such as tanks. Cobras destroyed more than 200 tanks and armored fighting vehicles during Operation Desert Storm.

Helicopters at Sea

Helicopters make ideal shipborne aircraft. They can take off and land using a small area. They are easier to store than fixed-wing aircraft. A helicopter can hover steadily in one place, even in high winds.

ABOVE AND BELOW THE WAVES

A Canadian Sea King prepares to drop a **sonar buoy** into the ocean, to listen for underwater intruders. Anti-submarine warfare (ASW) helicopters are not just passive observers. They can also drop mines and **depth charges** on enemy submarines.

FIRST UP, LAST DOWN

Every U.S. aircraft carrier has a rescue helicopter. It stands by to pick up crewmembers if an airplane misses the landing deck. This SH3 Sea King helicopter is the first up during missions or exercises and is the last to land.

>> **depth charge** – an underwater bomb triggered by water pressure

Heavy Lifters

Large helicopters carry out transport duties. They can deliver combat personnel and equipment close to the battlefront, without the need for a landing strip or airport.

ANYTHING, ANYWHERE

A CH54 Sky Crane helicopter prepares to lift a cargo container during the Vietnam War.

CHINOOK

The twin-rotor UH47 Chinook is a versatile transport helicopter with a large cargo area. It can land up to fourteen fully equipped combat troops in a small forest clearing.

>> **covert operations** – undercover missions, usually behind enemy lines

Coast Guard

The U.S. Coast Guard uses helicopters to patrol the U.S. coastline. The Coast Guard's job is to protect the shores and to assist people in distress.

SECURITY AT SEA

A Coast Guard HH60 Jayhawk patrols the ocean. The Jayhawk is a medium-range recovery helicopter, here fitted with an external stretcher.

SPECIAL OPERATIONS

Military helicopters have an important job in **covert operations**. They perform combat search-and-rescue (SAR) missions, resupply troops, and land army **Special Forces** behind enemy lines.

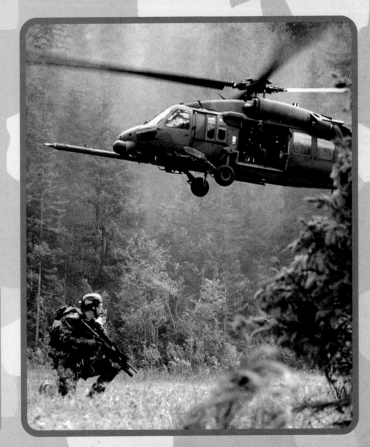

PAVE HAWK

An HH60 Pave Hawk pararescue helicopter contacts Special Forces behind enemy lines. The Pave Hawk can reach remote locations at night or in rough weather. It has a refueling probe for long-range operations.

Helicopter Heroes

Since the end of World War II, helicopters and the people who crew them have played an increasingly important part in conflicts. Legends have grown up around the actions of particular units and their crews.

PILOT SKILLS

Helicopters are not naturally **aerodynamic** and need constant "hands on" control. Pilots must have a high level of coordination. The pilot of this Canadian military H3 Sea King will also have to cope with rough seas, bad weather, and possible missile attack from surface vessels.

Korean War

The 3rd Air Rescue Squadron (ARS) went to Korea in 1950, after Communist North Korea invaded South Korea. Equipped with H5 and H19 helicopters, the search-and-rescue unit performed well. It located downed pilots behind enemy lines and flew wounded troops to field hospitals or hospital ships. The 3rd ARS alone was responsible for rescuing almost 10,000 United Nations (UN) personnel between June 1950 and July 1953. Many were behind enemy lines or in the ocean. For this heroism, the squadron earned three **Distinguished Unit citations**.

CHICKASAW

The legendary H19 Chickasaw, used by the 3rd ARS in Korea, also saw active service in Vietnam.

MOUNTAIN RESCUE

An Air Rescue H5 takes wounded U.S. Marines from Kari San mountain to field hospitals in the rear.

Kingbees

VIETNAM BEES

The **Kingbee** pilots stretched the limits of their Sikorsky H34 helicopters during the Vietnam War.

A view from the machine-gun position in the doorway of a Kingbee H34 showing another H34 behind. With their U.S.-built H34 and UH1 helicopters, the Kingbees of 219 Squadron, Vietnamese Air Force (VNAF), earned long-lasting respect from their allies. The Kingbees worked closely with U.S. Special Forces behind enemy lines.

FEARLESS

"I can name several targets where my team…. would be long gone without the Kingbees. Captains Tuong, Thinh, and Lieutenant Trong … were absolutely fearless."

U.S. Special Operations veteran,
Vietnam 1965–1975

Screaming Eagles

After Iraq invaded neighboring Kuwait, the legendary **Screaming Eagles** 101st Airborne Division sent a large force to take part in Operation Desert Storm. Their equipment included Apache and Black Hawk strike helicopters and Chinook transport helicopters. The 101st fired the first shots of the war from their Apaches, taking out Iraqi air defenses and bombing the Iraqi capital of Baghdad in January 1991.

DESERT STORM

An AH64 Apache strike helicopter in the desert mountains

MIDDLE EAST

Helicopter air traffic controllers direct takeoffs and landings onboard the USS *Essex*. The ship was taking part in anti-terrorist operations in the Middle East in 2002.

>> **Screaming Eagles** – so called for their screaming-eagle shoulder patch

Helicopter Weapons

The helicopter is a platform for many kinds of weapons systems, depending on the job it has to do. Strike helicopters are armed with missiles, rockets, and machine guns. Many navy helicopters carry assorted anti-submarine and anti-ship weapons.

TOW POWER

A German Army BO105 MBB Eurocopter armed with U.S.-built TOW **wire-guided** anti-armor missiles. Small and agile, it can sneak up on its prey quickly and quietly. This gives the target little time to take evasive action.

GUNS AND GRENADES

A technician checks the M134 7.62mm minigun and the M129 40mm grenade launcher on the AH1 Cobra. These weapons are located in the nose of the helicopter, below the pilot's cockpit.

>> wire-guided – a missile that is controlled by a wire from the launch tube

Hawk Family

The Sikorsky UH60 is a **utility helicopter** and also has an all-around combat role. It can be fitted with different weapons and equipment for ground attack, combat assault, or anti-ship missions.

SEAHAWK AND PENGUIN

A U.S. Navy Seahawk launches its Penguin anti-ship missile. Penguin is a heat-seeking, guided ship-to-ship missile made in Norway. Only the U.S. Navy is equipped with this helicopter-launched version.

BLACK HAWK

The Black Hawk is the U.S. Army version of the UH60. The Black Hawk can carry up to four external stores support system (ESSS) pods. They hold additional fuel and weapons for extended-range operations.

Rockets

Folding-Fin Aerial Rockets (FFARs) were developed for the U.S. Navy in the late 1940s. Modern rockets provide close air support. They are launched either from fixed-wing airplanes or rotorcraft.

HYDRA

An AH1 modernized Cobra fires a stream of 2.75-inch Hydra FFARs from ground level. These rockets can be used against light tanks or troops or for **smoke screening**.

SCOUT

A closeup of the SS-11 wire-guided missile rack on a British light reconnaissance helicopter

HELICOPTER GUNSHIP

A Russian-built Mi24 Hind Helicopter Gunship. Gunships provide a stable platform for **area denial** operations. They are equipped with massive firepower, using machine guns, missiles, rockets, and grenades to keep the enemy busy during an attack by ground or air forces.

Helicopter Missions

Helicopters can fly in rough weather and can land and take off using small spaces. They are ideal for rescue work and special operations. During the Korean War, helicopters found and flew the wounded to field hospitals. In the early 2000s, helicopters searched the mountains of Afghanistan for terrorists. Over time, the helicopter has proved to be a vital part of the military's hardware.

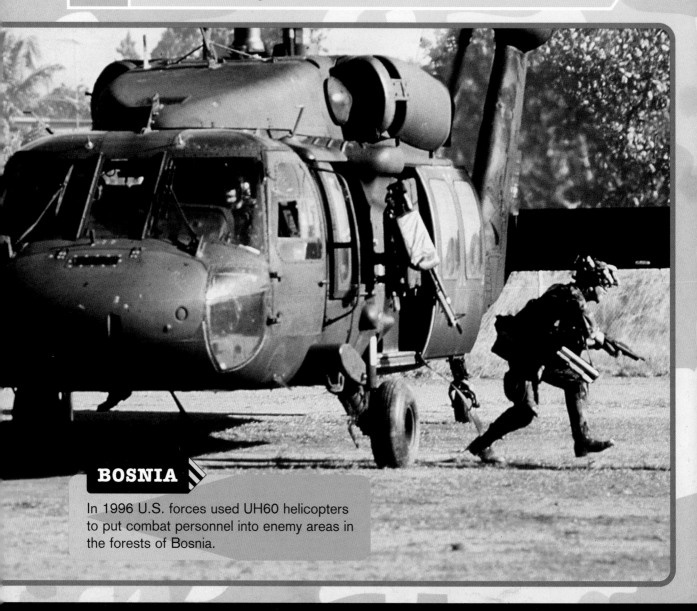

BOSNIA

In 1996 U.S. forces used UH60 helicopters to put combat personnel into enemy areas in the forests of Bosnia.

>> **evacuation** – removing wounded personnel from the battle zone

Field Hospitals

There was a shortage of helicopters during the Korean War. Their use for medical **evacuation** evolved over time. Some of the remote battle zones were up to 40 miles or more from the nearest Mobile Army Surgical Hospital (MASH). Helicopters provided a quick and smooth transit from battlefield to the hospital. They saved many lives that might otherwise have been lost had wounded been transported overland.

AIR AID

A wounded U.S. 21st Infantry soldier is lifted onto a helicopter for evacuation to a hospital in Korea, April 1951. Communist North Korea invaded South Korea in 1950 but retreated after UN forces stepped in.

CASEVAC CHOPPER

An 8225th MASH **casevac** helicopter team in Korea in October 1951. It has a full set of life-saving equipment to help the wounded.

Civilians in Distress

Helicopters often take part in civilian rescue operations. They can hover in bad weather over rough seas to pick up shipwrecked sailors or land in small mountain clearings to rescue lost climbers. Organizations like the U.S. Coast Guard, Air National Guard, and local rescue units save many lives.

UNLUCKY DAY

Saturday, January 13, 2001, was an unlucky day for a 14-year old mountain biker from California. The young man was separated from his brother in the Angeles National Forest. The Ventura County Search-and-Rescue helicopter was alerted, and a team flew out to find him. They found him alive and well after 48 hours in the open and airlifted him to safety.

SHIPWRECK RESCUE

A U.S. Coast Guard HH60 helicopter hovers above the deck of the passenger liner *Sea Breeze I*. In December 2000, the 600-foot ship was **foundering** in the Atlantic Ocean 300 miles off the coast of Virginia. The Coast Guard sent two HH60 search-and-rescue helicopters and two C130 Hercules airplanes to the scene. In heavy seas and high winds, 34 crewmembers were **winched** to safety before the ship finally sank.

LONG JOB

"... Finally, with a menacing cargo boom just five feet away from the helicopter's rotor blades, the pararescue man was lowered aboard the ship. It was ten minutes short of midnight. We had been on an alert since noon that day and now, almost 12 hours later, work was just beginning...."

Major James E. McArdle Jr, U.S. Air Force Rescue and Recovery Squadron, Korea

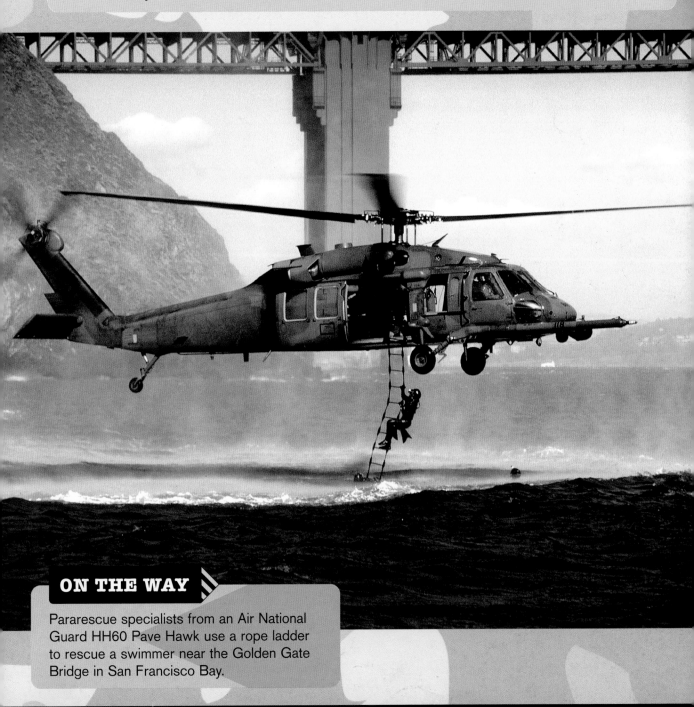

ON THE WAY

Pararescue specialists from an Air National Guard HH60 Pave Hawk use a rope ladder to rescue a swimmer near the Golden Gate Bridge in San Francisco Bay.

Long-Distance Recovery

Conflicts that affect the rest of the world can occur almost anywhere. So international peacekeeping forces have to operate at long distances. Airplanes and helicopters make such missions possible.

BOSNIA RESCUE

U.S. Air Force pilot Captain Scott O'Grady arrives at a U.S. airbase in Italy after his rescue. His F16 fighter jet was shot down on a UN mission over Bosnia in June 1995. A rescue operation was launched from the USS *Kearsarge*, using marine CH53 helicopters. After a week of avoiding enemy search parties, Captain O'Grady was finally located and flown back to safety.

53S STANDBY

Sea Stallion helicopters sit on the deck of USS *Kearsarge* in the Adriatic Sea.

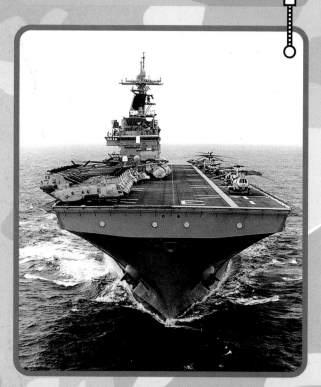

HEROES

"The people I want to thank ... are the men and women of the Navy and Marine Corps ... who came in there and saved me. If you want to find heroes, that's where to look."

Captain Scott O'Grady,
U.S. Air Force, June 1995

Enduring Freedom

Coalition helicopters were a vital factor in securing safe operating bases in Afghanistan in 2001 and 2002. Their arrival was just the beginning of a long international war against terrorism.

OPERATION ANACONDA

In May 2002, a ground crew unloaded a UH60 Black Hawk from a C17 Globemaster transport airplane. The operation to enclose and destroy **al-Qaeda** forces in Afghanistan would not have been possible without the support of both attack and transport helicopters.

Helicopter Skills

Fighting helicopters have very different characteristics from fixed-wing airplanes. They are slower, but they can hover and even fly backward. The pilots engaged in helicopter warfare make effective use of such differences.

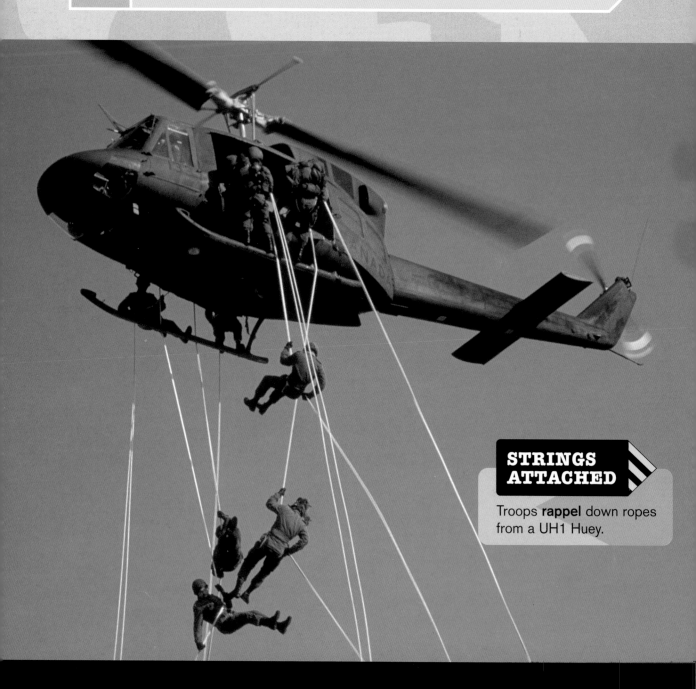

STRINGS ATTACHED

Troops **rappel** down ropes from a UH1 Huey.

VTOL

Vertical takeoff and landing (VTOL) gives the helicopter its edge. VTOL sets helicopters apart from most fixed-wing aircraft. The ability to hover in the air makes the helicopter ideal for covert and **reconnaissance** operations. A military helicopter often acts halfway between a combat aircraft and an armored fighting vehicle.

AEROBATIC

A French-built Aerospatiale Super Puma avoids contact with the enemy. Modern strike helicopters must be extremely easy to fly to avoid enemy missile fire.

HIDDEN THREAT

The Apache AH64 was designed to hide behind ground features. It can then pop up and fire its anti-tank missiles, before dropping down out of sight again. Ground features, such as forests, also absorb engine noise.

INVISIBLE ABOVE THE WAVES

A Seahawk lowers a sonar buoy into the sea. Hovering above the ocean, U.S. Navy ASW helicopters cannot be found by submarines.

Formations

Many rescue and attack missions are carried out using several helicopters together. This **tactic** increases the chance of success but also provides more **covering fire.** Sometimes, a "stand-off" helicopter is also added. It flies above and to one side of the group, acting as an airborne guardian.

OUTASIGHT

A German army Bell Jet Ranger leads, with an MBB105 light reconnaissance helicopter (*bottom*) as wingman. They are on ground-hugging combat air patrol (CAP).

TWO'S COMPANY

Helicopters frequently fly missions in pairs or combinations of pairs, with a leader and a wingman for cover. This basic formation is also used by fixed-wing aircraft.

> **tactic** =

Racetracks and Dogbones

A standard tactic is the L-attack. This involves a string of helicopters in an angled approach, intended to confuse enemy fire. The L-attack then develops into either a "dogbone" or "racetrack" pattern. With correct spacing, the helicopters can almost continuously shoot at the target. The dogbone allows an even spread of gunfire from each side of the aircraft. The racetrack keeps just one side facing the enemy, if only one side-gun is fitted.

SAFETY IN NUMBERS

A string of Pave Hawk helicopters approaches its target over mountainous terrain.

SLASHING ATTACK

"The L-attack is used for a slashing attack. The idea is that either en route to an insertion point or en route to a survivor you would encounter some opposition."

Lieutenant Commander J. Nordhill, U.S. Navy Helicopter Combat Support Squadron

Helicopter Enemies

Helicopters are less efficient at high altitudes than airplanes that have stationary wings, and they are not as quick to move around. These qualities make them easier to attack than other aircraft, especially from the ground.

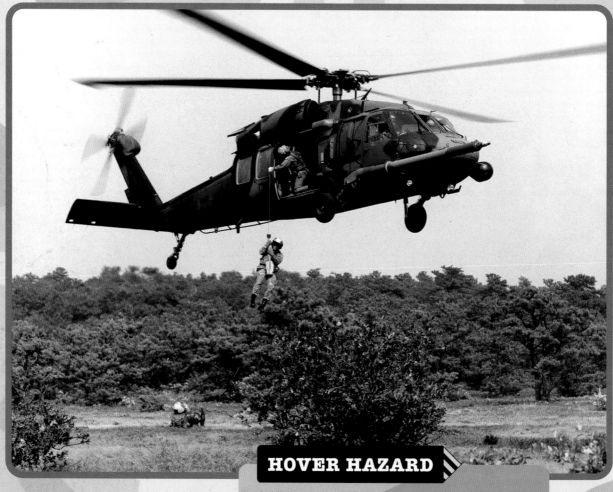

HOVER HAZARD

A UH60 hovers motionless in the air. It can train its guns or missiles on a target more accurately than a fast-moving airplane. But it also offers an easy target to enemy groundfire.

Missile Alert

Helicopters are bulky. Most do not have the **stealth** features of some modern combat airplanes. Their motors also push out a lot of heat, especially when hovering. Missiles that find their targets using radar or heat-seeking **infrared** are a potential threat.

AFV DEFENSES

Armored fighting vehicles, like tanks, are often targets for helicopter attack. They have defensive anti-helicopter weapons of their own. This U.S. LAV25 armored car is fitted with a TOW anti-tank missile launcher, which is also effective against low-flying helicopters.

INFANTRY WEAPONS

U.S. soldiers prepare to launch a Stinger anti-aircraft missile. Helicopters frequently operate at low levels. They are particularly easy targets for infantry weapons, such as machine guns and hand-held missiles and rockets.

Mechanical Failure

Helicopters are not aerodynamic. They rely on mechanical engineering to function. For this reason, they often require more maintenance. They are more likely to suffer mechanical breakdowns.

HANDS ON

A helicopter repair crew works on an Apache AH64 based in Afghanistan in 2002. Helicopter maintenance is a 24-hour, hands-on job.

Defenses

Low, slow, bulky, and likely to suffer from mechanical problems, helicopters might not seem ideal fighting machines. However, sophisticated electronic defenses and engine **sound baffles** help to restore the balance.

ECM

Electronic countermeasures (ECM) are essential to military helicopter security. The MH53J Pave Low helicopter is the most technologically advanced helicopter in the world. It has infrared, radar, and laser equipment to find and avoid enemy attack.

STEALTHY VTOL

Modern military helicopters are being developed with stealth in mind. Design technology used in the development of airplanes like the B2 and F117 stealth bombers is being adapted for strike helicopters like this Sikorsky RAH66.

Helicopter Parade

There are many different kinds of helicopters. Some are lightweight, **single-seat** reconnaissance and observation aircraft. Long-distance big lifters are also popular. Anti-submarine and anti-armor strike helicopters have recently joined the parade.

AH1 SUPER COBRA

The Super Cobra is a legend. It was first manufactured by Bell Helicopters, Inc., in 1966. The AH1 logged more than 1 million combat flying hours in Vietnam. The helicopter has seen more than thirty years of continuous development since that time.

Details:
Crew: 2
Length: 45 ft. 3 in.
Width: 10 ft. 9 in.
Propulsion: 2 x 1,690 hp **turboshaft** engines
Max Speed: 175 mph
Ceiling: 14,750 ft.
Armament: 1 x 20mm cannons, various missiles, rockets

SH60 SEA HAWK

The U.S. Army has the MH/UH53 Black Hawk. The Sea Hawk is the U.S. Navy's carrier-borne, anti-submarine, and search-and-rescue aircraft. It also carries cargo, is involved in special operations, and takes on radar reconnaissance tasks.

Details:
Crew: 3
Length: 50 ft
Width: 5 ft 6 in.
Propulsion: 2 x 1,662 hp turboshaft engines
Max Speed: 175 mph
Ceiling: 13,000 ft.
Armament: 2 x torpedoes, 1 x Penguin anti-ship missile

CH47 CHINOOK

The Chinook is a twin-engine, twin-rotor helicopter. It is designed for transporting troops, cargo, and weapons in all weather conditions. Development first began in 1961. The aircraft has been regularly upgraded since then.

Details:
Crew: 2
Length: 50 ft.
Width: 14 ft 9 in.
Propulsion: 2 x 1770 hp turboshaft engines
Max Speed: 167 mph
Ceiling: 10,000 ft.
Armament: 4,000 lb. external load

Helicopter Parade

DEFENDER 500

Boeing/McDonnell Douglas in the United States developed the Defender 500 to sell to foreign military forces. Many versions are available, including anti-tank, combat air support, and observation models.

Details:
Crew: 1–2
Length: 24 ft. 10 in.
Width: 6 ft. 3 in.
Propulsion: 1 x 375 hp turboshaft engine
Max Speed: 150 mph
Ceiling: 15,000 ft.
Armament: 2 x 7.62mm machine guns, Hydra rockets, Hellfire/TOW/Stinger missiles, grenade launchers

ROOIVALK CSH2 COMBAT HELICOPTER

The Rooivalk was developed by South Africa in 1998. It is equipped with air-to-air missiles, anti-tank missiles, and a rapid-fire cannon. It is designed to be hard to pick up on radar and has high resistance to damage.

Details:
Crew: 2
Length: 61 ft. 3 in.
Width: 10 ft.
Propulsion: 2 x 1845 hp turboshaft engines
Max Speed: 193 mph
Ceiling: 20,000 ft.
Armament: 1 x 20mm cannon, Mokopa anti-tank missiles, Mistral or Denel air-to-air missiles, **unguided rockets**

>> **unguided rocket** = a rocket that has no onboard guidance or control sy___em

MI24 HIND

The MI24 Hind is built in Russia. It is a combined combat-assault helicopter and helicopter-gunship. It was used extensively during the Soviet Union's war in Afghanistan in the 1980s.

Details:
Crew: 2
Length: 57 ft. 5 in.
Width: 10 ft.
Propulsion: 2 x 2,200 hp **turbines**
Max Speed: 168 mph
Ceiling: 15,000 ft.
Armament: 1 x 12.7mm machine gun,
  1 x 30mm cannon, anti-tank guided
  missiles, rockets, 2,200 lb. bomb load

turbine – a jet engine with turbine blades to increase power output

Helicopter Parade

PAH2 TIGER

The PAH2 Tiger is one of the most advanced combat helicopters in the world. It is jointly built by France and Germany and has many similarities to the AH64 Apache. The PAH2 can be adapted for a variety of strike and reconnaissance missions.

Details:
Crew: 2
Length: 46 ft. 3 in.
Width: 14 ft. 10 in.
Propulsion: 1 x MTR390 turboshaft
Max Speed: 179 mph
Ceiling: 12,000 ft.
Armament: 1 x 30mm machine gun, HOT anti-tank and Mistral anti-aircraft missiles, rockets

BELL UH1 IROQUOIS

The Iroquois is the most widely used utility helicopter in the world. The Bell UH1, nicknamed "Huey" (from its original U.S. Army designation HU1), was the workhorse of the Vietnam era. Current models are being upgraded for service with the U.S. Marine Corps.

Details:
Crew: 2–4
Length: 57 ft. 4 in.
Width: 6 ft. 2 in.
Propulsion: 1 x T400 turboshaft
Max Speed: 140 mph
Ceiling: 14,200 ft.
Armament: 7.62mm or .50 **caliber** machine guns, rockets

AH64 APACHE

The AH64 Apache is the U.S. Army's primary attack helicopter. Its fast-reaction airborne weapon system can fight up close to destroy, disrupt, or delay enemy forces. Its main weapon is the **Hellfire** anti-tank guided missile.

Details:
Crew: 2
Length: 58 ft. 3 in.
Width: 17 ft. 2 in.
Propulsion: 2 x T700 turboshaft engines
Max Speed: 145 mph
Ceiling: 12,000 ft.
Armament: 1 x 33mm machine gun,
  Hellfire anti-tank, Sidearm anti-radar,
  Sidewinder air-to-air missiles, rockets

Helicopter Parade

MH60 PAVE HAWK

The Sikorsky MH60 Pave Hawk is a twin-engine medium-lift helicopter operated by the U.S. Air Force Special Operations Command. Its main jobs are transporting Special Forces troops and conducting combat search-and-rescue missions. MH60s played a major part in Operation Desert Storm in 1991 and in Afghanistan in 2001 and 2002.

Details:
Crew: 4
Length: 64 ft. 8 in.
Width: 5 ft. 6 in.
Propulsion: 2 x 1630 hp T700 turboshaft engines
Max Speed: 184 mph
Ceiling: 19,000 ft.
Armament: 2 x 7.62mm miniguns

> light ut

SA341 GAZELLE

The Gazelle is a French-built **light utility** helicopter. It can be adapted for anti-tank and anti-helicopter tasks, as well as light transport and training. It is used by more than 20 countries worldwide.

Details:
Crew: 1–2
Length: 31 ft. 3 in.
Width: 6 ft. 6 in.
Propulsion: 1 x 590 hp turboshaft engine
Max Speed: 193 mph
Ceiling: 16,000 ft.
Armament: 7.62mm machine guns and/or 20mm cannon, anti-tank and anti-aircraft missiles, rockets

AS565 PANTHER/DAUPHIN

The Panther is a military version of France's Aerospatiale Dauphin. It is used by many countries, including the U.S. Coast Guard.

Details:
Crew: 2–3
Length: 37 ft. 6 in.
Width: 7 ft. 6 in.
Propulsion: 2 x **Turbomeca** turboshaft engines
Max Speed: 170 mph
Ceiling: 10,200 ft.
Armament: rockets, anti-tank missiles

>> **Turbomeca**

Future Helicopters

The next generation of helicopters and VTOL aircraft will have greater stealth and more **avionics.** They will not require as much maintenance time.

COMANCHE

The Boeing–Sikorsky RAH66 is the U.S. Army's armed reconnaissance helicopter for the next generation. It will replace the AH1 Super Cobra and OH58 Warrior reconnaissance helicopters and will supplement the AH64 Apache.

FASTER, MEANER, LEANER

The Comanche will have more powerful motors than the Apache or Warrior. It will be able to carry more missiles and will be harder to find either on radar or by eye.

>> **avionics** = aviation electronics, such as navigation equipment

Tilt-rotor Technology

Aircraft manufacturers have been experimenting with **tilt-rotor airplanes** for several decades. The advantage lies in being able to combine the best of both fixed-wing aircraft and VTOL aircraft. Despite setbacks, the tilt-rotor aircraft is probably the future for military medium transport.

OSPREY

The V22 Osprey is an experimental tilt-rotor slated to replace the Vietnam-era transport helicopters of the U.S. Marine Corps. The Osprey can fly like a normal airplane. It can also land and take off from a small platform or unpaved area.

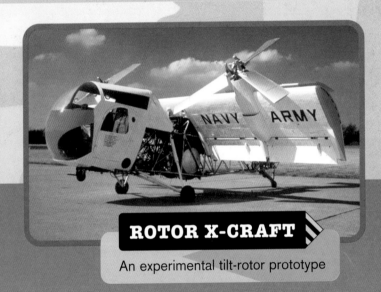

ROTOR X-CRAFT

An experimental tilt-rotor prototype

STOP-GO STORY

After several fatal accidents during trials, the V22 project was put on hold in 2000. In May 2002, however, tests resumed. The motors can rotate, pointing upward for vertical operation and forward for horizontal flight.

tilt-rotor airplane — an aircraft with propellers that can also be rotors

Future Helicopters

Reducing the number of mechanical parts is an important part of future helicopter design. This will reduce wear and tear and high maintenance costs. Replacing the tail anti-torque rotor with something simpler is one solution.

UNMANNED ROTORCRAFT

The U.S. Army began research into **UAV** rotorcraft in 2002. Reduced weight and no pilot means lower costs and less risk to personnel. UAVs could act as reconnaissance aircraft. They could also provide support to manned helicopters, such as the Apache or the new Comanche strike aircraft.

HUMMINGBIRD

The A160 Hummingbird is an unmanned **surveillance** and targeting rotorcraft project. The lightweight vehicle will remain airborne for up to 48 hours without refueling.

Nose section can be changed to make room for different types of equipment

Control aerial

Foldable landing gear with 33-inch ground clearance to allow space for extra aerials or other items

AIR SCOOTER

This experimental one-person heliscooter has attracted some military interest. It could provide combat troops with extra mobility. The aircraft has fan rotors that can be tilted to change direction, with a handgrip throttle to control speed and lift.

Hardware at a Glance

AA = anti-aircraft
AIM = air interception missile
ARS = Air Rescue Squadron
ASRAAM = advanced short-range air-to-air missile
ASW = anti-submarine warfare
CAP = combat air patrol
ECM = electronic countermeasures
ESSS = external stores support system

FFAR = folding-fin aerial rocket
MASH = Mobile Army Surgical Hospital
MRCA = multirole combat aircraft
SAR = search and rescue
TOW = tube-launched, optically-tracked, wire-guided
UAV = unmanned aerial vehicle
VTOL = vertical takeoff and landing

Further Reading & Websites

Angelucci, Enzo. *The Illustrated Encyclopedia of Military Aircraft*. New York: Book Sales, 2001.

Budd, E. S. *Military Helicopters (Machines at Work)*. Plainview, NY: Enslow Publishing, 2001.

Holden, Henry M. *Black Hawk Helicopter (Aircraft)*. Berkeley Heights, NJ: Enslow Publishing, 2001.

Holden, Henry M. *Navy Combat Aircraft and Pilots (Aircraft)*. Berkeley Heights, NJ: Enslow Publishing, 2002.

Loves, June. *Military Aircraft (Flight)*. Broomall, PA: Chelsea House, 2001.

Norman, C.J. *Military Helicopters*. London: Franklin Watts, 1989.

Rendall, David. *Jane's Aircraft Recognition Guide*. New York: HarperCollins, 1999.

Sullivan, George. *Modern Combat Helicopters (Military Aircraft)*. New York: Facts on File, 1986.

Taylor, Mike. *Air Forces of World War II (World War II)*. Edina, MN: Abdo & Daughters, 1998.

Air Force Link <http://www.af.mil>
Bell Helicopters Textron <http://www.bellhelicopter.textron.com>
Center of Military History <http://www.army.mil/cmh-pg>
Commemorative Air Force <http://www.commemorativeairforce.org>
DefenseLink <http://www.defenselink.mil>
Federation of American Scientists <http://www.fas.org/man.index.html>
Helispot Photos <http://www.helispot.com>
NATO multimedia <http://www.nato.int>
Sikorsky <http://www.sikorsky.com>
U.S. Marine Corps <http://www.usmc.mil>
U.S. Navy <http://www.usn.mil>

Places to Visit

You can see examples of some of the helicopters and other rotorcraft contained in this book by visiting the military and aviation museums listed here.

American Airpower Heritage Museum, Midland, TX <www.airpowermuseum.org>
American Helicopter Museum & Education Center, West Chester, PA
   <www.helicoptermuseum.org>
Army Aviation Museum, Fort Rucker, Ozark, AL <www.armyavnmuseum.org>
Canadian Warplane Heritage Museum, Hamilton Airport, Mount Hope, Ontario
   <www.warplane.com>
Hiller Aviation Museum, San Carlos, CA <www.hiller.org>
Kenosha Military Museum, Pleasant Prairie, WI <www.kenoshamilitarymuseum.com>
National Museum of Naval Aviation, Pensacola, FL <www.naval-air.org>
RCAF Memorial Museum, Trenton, Ontario <www.rcafmuseum.on.ca>
San Diego Aerospace Museum, San Diego, CA <www.aerospacemuseum.org>
Smithsonian National Air and Space Museum, Washington, D.C. <www.wash.si.edu>
U.S. Air Force Museum, Wright-Patterson AFB, OH <www.wpafb.af.mil/museum/>
Valiant Air Command Warbird Museum, Titusville, FL <www.vacwarbirds.org>
War Eagles Air Museum, Santa Teresa, NM <www.war-eagles-air-museum.com>
Western Canada Aviation Museum, Winnipeg, Manitoba <www.wcam.mb.ca>

Index

Picture Sources

Boeing; 36 (t)
Corel; 4, 7, 9, 10, 11 (t), 12, 16 (t), 27, 28, 35 (b), 39, 41, 43
Defense Visual Information Center; 6, 7 (b), 13, 14, 15, 16 (b), 17 (b), 18, 21, 25, 26, 29, 30, 32, 33, 34, 38 (b), 45
EADS; 38 (t)
John Batchelor; 5, 35 (t)
M K Dartford; 19 (t)
Robert Hunt Library; 5 (t)

Sikorsky; 33 (b), 42
U.S. Air Force; 8, 19 (b), 23, 24 (t), 33 (t), 37 (b), 40
U.S. Army; 11 (b), 20
U.S. Coast Guard, 22 (b)
U.S. Marine Corps;
U.S. Navy; 9, 17 (t), 24 (b)